SIMPLY CONNECT

Morning and Evening Prayers for 31 Days

ARCHIE BUIE

The Peppertree Press
Sarasota, Florida

Design by: Elizabeth K. Peters

For information regarding permission,
Call 941-922-2662 or contact us at our website:
www.peppertreepublishing.com or write to:
the Peppertree Press, LLC.
Attention: Publisher
1269 First Street, Suite 7
Sarasota, Florida 34236

ISBN: 978-0-9822540-1-1
Library of Congress Number: 2008942021

Printed in the U.S.A.
Printed December 2008

DEDICATED TO ...

Carolyn, Maribeth, Ben & Karen,
and my mother, Genevieve

Special thanks to Nell Thrift
for the initial editing of my prayers
and for the invaluable assistance
of my wife, Carolyn, and my daughter, Maribeth

❀

"Prayer is [our] most accessible means to the greatest possible power. Not only can we bring about a whole new world through prayer but one's own life can by its means become astonishingly new."

Nels F.S. Ferré
Strengthening the Spiritual Life

"Prayer is relationship. It is being with God. It is meeting. It is a personal relationship in which you and God move from a hello of politeness to an embrace of love. It is communion. All other dimensions of prayer must take second place to this primary dimension."

Maxie Dunnam
The Workbook of Living Prayer

"God doesn't want us to pile up impressive phrases. He doesn't want us to use words without thinking about their meaning. He wants us simply to talk to him as to a friend or father – authentically, reverently, personally, earnestly."

Bill Hybels
Too Busy Not To Pray

"Keep on asking, and you will receive what you ask for. Keep on seeking, and you will find. Keep on knocking and the door will be opened to you. For everyone who asks, receives. Everyone who seeks, finds. And to everyone who knocks, the door will be opened."

Words of Jesus
Matthew 7:7-8, New Living Translation

Note to Reader

As you explore your relationship with God, allow these prayers to serve as a catalyst in your experience with Him. May these prayers help you come to know God in a deeper way, strengthen your daily prayer life, and encourage you to evaluate your life's journey.

This book is based on the simple format of a prayer for each morning and each evening for 31 days (one month). The prayers can be used successively and then repeated, or you may focus on certain prayer topics as they relate to your specific situation. As you work through this book, use the blank facing pages to jot down notes, reflections, persons to pray for, and any prayer requests that you may have.

A couple of Sunday prayers are included in the Appendix to be used as you choose. You will also find prayers by Mother Teresa, Bishop Walter J. Carey, Dietrich Bonhoeffer, and Saint Francis of Assisi and the 17th Century Nun's Prayer, which have been meaningful to me.

May this book of prayers enable you to connect with God and grow in your relationship with Him.

ARCHIE BUIE

Morning and Evening
Prayers for 31 Days

DAY 1   NOTES, REFLECTIONS, PRAYER REQUESTS

POSSIBILITY

God of love, on my worst days life can get me down and leave me feeling discouraged and dissatisfied. Things don't go as I had planned, and people don't respond the way I thought they would. I become frustrated. I begin to question myself and lose my confidence.

When this occurs, don't let me give in to the negative.
Keep me open.
Keep me positive.
Keep me close to you.

Help me to make the best of this day, no matter what happens.
Let me bloom where I'm planted.
Expand my vision to see possibility.
Use my gifts and abilities for good.
Show me how to deal with each person
  you put in my path.
Lift me up, and enable me to stand straight and tall.

Lord, I don't know what this day will hold for me. But, I know I can place myself in your hands and that you will be faithful and true in every circumstance. In Jesus' name. Amen.

DAY 1   NOTES, REFLECTIONS, PRAYER REQUESTS

CARE

God, it amazes me that you hear my prayers, that you love me, and that you care about my life. To you I'm not just a number. I'm not simply alone in the universe, but I am one of your magnificent creations and my life has value and meaning. Even more than that, you love me! Thank you, Lord, for being a good and loving God and for being there for me day after day.

At times, I wonder how you think I'm doing with the life you've given me.

I recall
the words I said today,
the silences I kept,
the decisions I made.

Was I obedient to you?
Did my actions honor you?
Was my witness faithful and true?
Did I reflect your love and caring?

As I prepare for sleep, I ask that I may leave these pressing questions in your hands and any worries I have over them. I thank you for tomorrow and the chance to begin again. Create in me a new heart and a right spirit.

As sleep comes, I surrender my life to you and place my family, my friends, and myself in your care. Amen.

DAY 2   NOTES, REFLECTIONS, PRAYER REQUESTS

JOY

To you, God, I sing my happiest song of praise. To you I whistle my most joyful tune. To you I lift my heart in gratitude, for you love me as if I were the only one to love. Help me to claim that love and to become more loving in the process.

As I begin this new day, take away any fear within me, and let me live with joy and confidence. Even when things go wrong, let me not lose heart, but keep believing, keep trusting you, keep living life.

I know that today I will meet those who have lost their way, those who are down and out, those who have been crushed by some changing circumstance or who may be angry or upset from some experience of living. Lord, let me reach out to every person with love and concern. Reveal your love and caring through me. Help me to encourage more than I push away.

Into this beautiful, yet often troubled world, let your peace come to all people – both near and far, and teach me to do my part. In Jesus' name. Amen.

Blessed are the peacemakers,
for they will be called children of God.   Matthew 5:9

DAY 2   NOTES, REFLECTIONS, PRAYER REQUESTS

LIGHT

Lord, it has been a good but long day. I'm tired. I'm worn out from all I experienced today. I have little energy left, and it's night. Things seem heavier and more brooding at night. At night my faith doesn't seem as strong; my thoughts are not as focused. Some nights I can easily get off track and begin feeling a little down.

I need your assurance. Let me remember that the darkness doesn't affect your love for me at all. You love me throughout the day and throughout the night without condition. You are more powerful than the darkness. You created the darkness, and you rule over it.

So, dear God, I again give you my heart and my life. Remove whatever darkness there is within me. Especially take away the darkness of sin and doubt, and fill my life with your redeeming light, the warm, penetrating light of Jesus.

Even in the night let me feel your calming presence near and know that I am safe and secure. I ask these things in the name of Him who overcame the darkness and is my light forever. Amen.

The light shines in the darkness, and the
darkness has never put it out. John 1:5

DAY 3   NOTES, REFLECTIONS, PRAYER REQUESTS

AWARE

Mighty God, you know my heart. You know my thoughts.
You know my strengths. You know my weaknesses.

As I begin this new day, let me begin it with you. No matter
where I have been or how I have lived, let me welcome and
appreciate this day. It's clean and fresh with no mistakes in
it. Let me receive this gift from you and honor you in the
way I live it.

Don't let me waste it.
Don't let me abuse it.
Don't let me treat it carelessly.
Don't let me just go through the motions.

Help me to get outside of myself.
Sharpen my awareness and sensitize my heart.
Open my eyes to the needs of those around me—
the lonely,
the fearful,
the hurting,
the reluctant,
the desperate,
the unappreciated,
the misunderstood,
those who are like lost sheep in the world.

As I step out into this new day, Lord, let it be a good day—
a day of loving and serving in your most holy name. Amen.

DAY 3   NOTES, REFLECTIONS, PRAYER REQUESTS

FORGET

As I reflect on the day, Lord, I lift up my heart to you in praise and thanksgiving. You watched over my life. You led me through the day.

But I confess that sometimes
I forget that you are with me through your Holy Spirit.
I forget to pray unless there is an emergency or crisis.
I forget to read your living Word.
I forget to be your witness in the words I speak and in the way
    I treat my family, my friends, my co-workers, and others.
I forget to seek your guidance in the big and little things.
I forget to share my day with you - my frustrations,
  my problems, my concerns, my successes, and my joys.
I forget to thank you for the blessings I receive.

Forgive me, and help me to do better. I still have much to learn and much to overcome. Thank you for loving me.

In your accepting love, let me be still now. Let me rest in the certainty that you are for me and with me and I need not be afraid. In the name of the One who came to save me. Amen.

DAY 4   NOTES, REFLECTIONS, PRAYER REQUESTS

VALUES

O Lord, you search me and you know me,
you know my resting and my rising,
you discern my purpose from afar.
You mark when I walk or lie down,
all my ways lie open to you.
O search me, God, and know my heart.
O test me and know my thoughts.
See that I follow not the wrong path
and lead me in the path of life eternal.   Psalm 139:1-3, 23-24

Father, I'm glad that you see into my heart even though I'm not proud of all that is there. Please work with me through this day so that I may avoid doing things that are not pleasing to you.

Keep me from being self-centered; help me to put you first. Teach me to be more generous with my time and my possessions. Enable me to keep my values high and my priorities straight.

When my patience wears thin, help me not to give in.
When my energy runs low, supply me with new strength.
When my nerves become frayed, give me calmness of mind.
When I run into conflict, give me wisdom to handle it well.
When I encounter a problem, help me to work through it.
When I become frustrated, enable me to persist and not
get bogged down.
When despair reaches out and tries to grab hold, let me rise above it.

Lord, this is the day that you have made, let me rejoice
and be glad in it! Amen.

DAY 4   NOTES, REFLECTIONS, PRAYER REQUESTS

RUN

God, as the day comes to an end, I think about the way I lived it out. I succeeded in some things and fell short in other things. Encourage me in the way that I need to live. Help me not to fall back into my old ways, but to move ahead with you at the center.

I thank you for the good-
> For beauty,
> For joy,
> For love,
> For opportunities to help and to serve,
> For...
> For...

Forgive me for the things that got in the way-
> My impatience,
> My lack of thankfulness,
> My procrastination,
> My ...
> My ...

As the days come and go, give me strength and courage to remain faithful to you as I run the race that is set before me. To your loving care, Father, I now entrust all those who are dear to me, especially...

Comfort those who are grieving this night, and wrap your loving arms around those who feel afraid or alone. We all need you, Lord. I give myself into your care and keeping. Through Jesus Christ. Amen.

DAY 5   NOTES, REFLECTIONS, PRAYER REQUESTS

NEW

Lord of life, thank you for the gift of this exquisite new day. It comes quietly, like a hidden treasure waiting to be discovered and celebrated. Open my eyes to everything it offers. Let me focus clearly on what this uncluttered day will bring.

Let me greet it with a happy heart.
Let my smiles outnumber my frowns.
Let my compliments outnumber my criticisms.
Let my caring be greater than my indifference.
Let my faith be larger than my doubt.
Let my generosity be bigger than my selfishness.

Let me give kindness and respect to persons I'll be with.
Let me face each difficulty with calmness and courage.

Make me more trusting of you,
Make me more open to your leading.

I know these are not easy tasks to accomplish. Help me to commit myself completely to each one, and I shall give you all the praise and glory. Amen.

DAY 5   NOTES, REFLECTIONS, PRAYER REQUESTS

LIFE

Loving God, I retreat from the noise of the world as I seek your presence, as I seek to open my heart to you. All day long I have been on the go; now, in the stillness of these moments, I look at my life.

On my best days
I'm happy and fulfilled,
brave and confident,
eager and hopeful,
full of life and ready for tomorrow.

On my worst days
I can become blue and regretful,
timid and unsure,
dull and pessimistic,
withdrawn and fearful of the future.

Lord, help me to focus on the best and highest that you offer. Keep my vision clear and my heart pure. Show me the way I need to live and let me not be distracted by the things of the world. You see and know me as I am. Make me as you desire me to be.

Now, God, give my body and my mind refreshing rest and renewal through this night. In the name of Jesus Christ, my Lord. Amen.

DAY 6   Notes, Reflections, Prayer Requests

INTEGRITY

Lord, as I go through this day, let me live it with integrity. Let me be honest and truthful in what I think, in what I say, and in what I do. Enable me to be up front and transparent in my interaction with others. Let me be true to my word and to you.

If I am tempted
    To look the other way,
    To compromise my values,
    To say one thing and do another,
    To take unethical shortcuts,
    To indulge in malicious gossip,
    To lie,
    To cheat,
    To judge others,
    To take advantage of someone,
    To make promises I can't keep,
    Help me to stand firm, to be strong, and not to give in.

Enable me to be the kind of person who does what is right and good. Equip me with unfaltering courage, and keep me mindful of your presence with me. In Jesus' name. Amen.

Blessed are the pure in heart, for they shall see God.
Matthew 5:8

DAY 6   NOTES, REFLECTIONS, PRAYER REQUESTS

Refresh

God, I come to this part of the day weak and weary from living. I did my best. I gave my all. I loved and cared. I lived responsibly. I was faithful to you. But the day's activities have taken their toll, and now I'm feeling depleted and diminished.

So, Lord, I ask you to
> Renew my mind,
> Refresh my hope,
> Rekindle my love,
> Resupply my faith,
> Replenish my energy,
> Restore my body.

Even with its problems, pressures, and challenges, life is good and I enjoy and appreciate the adventure of living. Thank you, God!

Through this night, uphold me with your Spirit and quiet any anxiety or restlessness I may feel. I entrust my loved ones, my friends, my enemies, and myself to your loving care, through Jesus Christ my Lord. Amen.

DAY 7   NOTES, REFLECTIONS, PRAYER REQUESTS

GUIDE

Gracious God, even though I am sitting still, my heart is beating and my mind is racing - thinking, planning, dreaming, and hoping for the best kind of day.

Calm my thoughts and open me to your presence. The day that lies ahead can only be the best if I put myself in your hands. In all that I undertake make your will known to me. Direct my efforts in the most productive path. Guide me in each situation.

As I prepare for this day, I ask you to care for
    those who are down and out,
    those who are friendless,
    those who have lost their passion and purpose,
    those who have become weak in body through
        surgery, accident, illness, or aging,
    those who are going through a time of crisis,
    those who are feeling desperate and confused,
    those whose lives have been shattered by loss.

Lord, show me how to express care and concern to the people that are a part of my day. Let me take no one for granted.

My needs are great, but you are greater still. Let your kingdom come through me, today and forever. Amen.

DAY 7   NOTES, REFLECTIONS, PRAYER REQUESTS

UNFINISHED

As the shadows lengthen and the night comes, I open my heart and mind to your presence, Lord.

You know how I lived today.

There were times
That I kept silent when I should have spoken up
and spoke up when I should have kept silent.

That I held back when I should have acted
and acted when I should have held back.

That I talked about the faults of others
and avoided seeing my own faults.

That I got upset about little things that didn't matter
and had little passion about things that could really
make a difference.

In hindsight I can see what I should have said and what I should have done. Forgive me. Don't let me give up on myself. Keep working with me - making me more loving, more patient, more understanding. Like a carpenter with a piece of unfinished wood, keep shaping my life into the person you want me to be. That's what I hope for.

As I enter this time of sleep let me relax and rest in your bountiful mercy and your never-ending love. Amen.

DAY 8   NOTES, REFLECTIONS, PRAYER REQUESTS

SURRENDER

God, into this world of highs and lows you come with your unshakable love and your life-giving power. Whatever this day will bring, help me face it with undaunted courage and daring faith. Give me light for the journey and strength for the day.

Like a shepherd, go ahead of me to guide me, to protect me, to uphold me with your love. I willingly follow you, and give you my love, my obedience, my service, my witness, and my faithfulness.

Let me not be discouraged or fearful when things don't go my way. Instead, help me to trust you.

Make me aware of those around me. Give me a Christ-like heart to love, to care, and to reach out to those that will come into my life today.

> As the seed surrenders to the ground,
> As the sail surrenders to the wind,
> As the clay surrenders to the potter,
> Let me give myself freely and joyfully to you.

In the name of Him who stilled the wind and calmed the sea, I pray. Amen.

DAY 8   NOTES, REFLECTIONS, PRAYER REQUESTS

ABUNDANCE

Creator and Sustainer of all things, some nights I don't know what to say to you, but then I remember what your servant, Paul, said, *In everything give thanks.** So, Lord, I thank you for this day that is nearly over.

I am grateful
> For the beauty of the earth,
> For the freedoms I cherish,
> For your constant goodness,
> For good health and healing,
> For times of play and renewal,
> For guiding and sustaining my life,
> For work that requires my best effort,
> For challenges that cause me to grow,
> For family and friends to share life with.

You supply my every need. You fill my life with abundance. I can depend on you. You never let me down, and you give me hope for the future. You are always there for me. You carefully watch over my life and the lives of those I love. Thank you, Lord, for being so good and so gracious to me.

Now, let me sleep through the night with the assurance that I am in the very center of your steadfast love. Amen.

*I Thessalonians 5:18

DAY 9   NOTES, REFLECTIONS, PRAYER REQUESTS

BRIDGES

I'm ready, God, for this day that you have made, and I pray that it's ready for me.   As I go into the day, use me to build bridges instead of walls - bridges of love and caring, rather than walls of hatred and indifference.

> It's so easy just not to care, to enclose myself
> in my own little private world--insulated and isolated
> from everyone, surrounded by a wall of selfishness.

> It's so easy not to give love, to simply put up a prickly
> wall of dislike and distrust.   I decide not to give love,
> so I don't receive much love in return, and my heart
> becomes icy cold.

But you call me to love without condition, with no strings attached. So let the walls come down! Help me pull down the barriers I've erected, and teach me to love freely. As I live this day let me take the risk of caring – wall-free living!

Let me recognize every person as someone of value and worth, someone to be loved, respected, and appreciated. Help me to see beyond their walls of shyness, fear, indifference, insecurity, inadequacy, and pain. Use me to build bridges of love, and let the walls come tumbling down. For Jesus' sake. Amen.

DAY 9   NOTES, REFLECTIONS, PRAYER REQUESTS

CHANGE

Today has about come to an end, God. You led me through it and I thank you for it. You enabled me to do some good, and good things came my way. But as I look back over it, I confess that I should have done some things differently.

I should have loved more;
I should have laughed more;
I should have listened more intently;
I should have been more trusting of you;
I should have been more of an encourager;
I should have been more patient with people;
I should have given more of myself to others.

How did you see me, Lord?
Impatient,
Critical,
Judgmental,
Indifferent,
Uncaring?

I know that you want what is best for me, and you know the kind of person I am. I'm coming along, but I have a long way to go. Keep changing me from the inside out, and make me into the person you would have me be.

Now give me a quiet and peaceful night of refreshing rest. In the name of Jesus. Amen.

CONTROL

Living Lord, I am drawn to you as flowers are drawn to the sun. I seek to be your willing servant. Open my eyes, my ears, and my heart to your transforming Spirit, and to the needs of those around me.

At times, I can easily become
    Self-absorbed,
    Self-sufficient,
    Self-dominated.
I try to take control and live only for myself.

As you know, when that happens life begins to unravel, and it becomes a shallow and empty thing lacking in joy and goodness.

As I live this new day, help me to leave self behind and to focus on serving you and others. Let me walk in your way, not my way. Enable me to continually give up control, to surrender my life to you, and to trust you to guide me. In the name of Jesus. Amen.

For whoever would save his life will lose it, and whoever loses his life for my sake will find it.   Matthew 16:25

DAY 10   NOTES, REFLECTIONS, PRAYER REQUESTS

PRESENCE

Loving God, as this day nears its end I turn to you with a joyful and thankful heart. I praise you for the gift of life and the wonder of your love. I have so much! You bless me beyond measure, and yet I realize that many live in much harder situations.

Give strength and care
    to those who will go to bed hungry,
    to those who are homeless,
    to those whose lives have been turned upside down
    by some upset, crisis, or tragedy,
    to those who have lost a job,
    to those who suffer from health problems,
    to those dealing with an addiction,
    to those engaged in military conflict,
    to those who are oppressed,
    to those living without freedom,
    to those who have been shattered by loss,
    to those who are persecuted for their faith.

Now, God, settle my mind as I lie down to rest. Whether awake or asleep, I am happy knowing that I am still in your presence. Let me not be bothered by anxious thoughts or disturbing dreams. Let me sleep soundly, and awake refreshed and ready for a new day. To you be all the glory. Amen.

DAY 11   NOTES, REFLECTIONS, PRAYER REQUESTS

CHOICE

Mighty Creator, this day comes as a gift, freely given and to be freely received - bright shining sun, blue sky, soft white clouds, air to breathe, and fresh possibilities. Thank you, God, for this lovely new day. You've given me a choice - I can use the day's hours productively or begrudgingly. Help me to use them wisely and well.

Let me give more than I take.
Let me love more than I hate.
Let me trust more than I fear.
Let me laugh more than I cry.
Let me listen more than I talk.
Let me pray more than I worry.
Let me help more than I hinder.
Let me believe more than I question.
Let me build up more than I tear down.
Let me encourage more than I criticize.
Let me reach out more than I hold back.

As I prepare to leave this quiet place, give me a sense of your power and your glory, then let your Spirit guide me wherever I shall go. I ask these things in the name of Jesus. Amen.

DAY 11 NOTES, REFLECTIONS, PRAYER REQUESTS

GRACE

God, on the outside I may appear to have it all together, but on the inside I'm anything but that. You know how I am. Sometimes I'm clear about what needs to be done; the next moment I'm wishy-washy. Sometimes I'm full of faith; the next moment I'm wrestling with doubt and uncertainty. Sometimes I'm a good person doing right, and other times I'm a sinful person doing wrong.

If I allow it, sin can destroy more and more of the goodness within me. It can compromise my values, break down my faith in you, weaken my convictions, and gradually take me away from you, from Jesus, and all that is good.

Set me free from the chains that bind me. Release me from any wrongdoing that I have committed in my thoughts, in my words, or in my actions.

Lord, I know I cannot save myself. The only thing that can save me is your amazing grace – your unmerited love. Tonight let me receive and experience this free and gracious gift. I open my heart to you, and I invite you to come into my life and reclaim me as your very own.

Forgive me for the wrongs I have done, and make me a new and whole person on the inside. Now, let me sleep in peace this night knowing that I am loved by you. In the name of Jesus, my Savior. Amen.

DAY 12   NOTES, REFLECTIONS, PRAYER REQUESTS

REJOICE

Loving Creator, who made all things as they are, and called them good, give me today a mind and heart to rejoice in your creation.

I thank you for the world around me
for shrub and tree and flower and grass,
for the beauty of flowing rivers and the ocean blue,
for sun and moon and night and stars,
for family who know me best and love me still,
for friends who love and nurture me,
for the joy of youth and the richness of maturity,
for honest work and joyous play,
for foods that sustain my body,
for Bibles and creeds and songs of praise and prayers.

I thank you, Lord, for being there for me,
for being my hope when darkness tries to overtake me,
for being my strength when I am weak and uncertain,
for being my guide when the way ahead is unclear,
for being my comfort when I am afraid or upset,
for being my Savior when I feel lost or alone.

Go with me into this glorious day. May I know, really know, that your loving presence surrounds me and that your Holy Spirit guides me. In the name of your Son. Amen.

DAY 12   NOTES, REFLECTIONS, PRAYER REQUESTS

LOVE

Lord, you command us to love one another. It's so difficult at times - to love as you love. I look at my way of loving, and it is sometimes so selective and so limited. I often love people on my own terms. If they don't respond as I think they should, I give them the cold shoulder and quit loving them.

I want to love more deeply.

Show me how to give love without condition to those in my family, to my friends, to my co-workers, and to every person that comes into my life.

Tonight I think of those who need more love -
Family members...
Those I work with...
My friends...

Lord, enable me to keep giving love even when it is not returned.

I also pray for those persons in my life who are hard to love...
Teach me how to care for them.

Father, I entrust each of these persons into your loving care. Help me love them as I would like to be loved. In Jesus' name. Amen.

You have heard that it was said, 'You shall love your neighbor and hate your enemy.' But I say to you, 'Love your enemies and pray for those who persecute you...'

Matthew 5:43-44

DAY 13   NOTES, REFLECTIONS, PRAYER REQUESTS

FAITH

God, guide me as I go forth to live this day. Let me go with a willing spirit and an open heart.

Take away my fears:
Fear of failing,
Fear of making a mistake,
Fear of not being good enough,
Fear of the past,
Fear of the unknown,
Fear of dying.

Take away my worries:
Worry about what I have done,
Worry over what I have left undone,
Worry about my health,
Worry about what this world is coming to,
Worry about making ends meet,
Worry about what the future holds.
I worry about things I shouldn't worry about.
Forgive me.

Lord, I have absolute confidence in you. You abundantly provide for my needs, and there is no reason for me to fear or worry. In that assurance, let me live this day with audacious faith! In the Savior's name. Amen.

DAY 13   NOTES, REFLECTIONS, PRAYER REQUESTS

LIVING

Today I put in my time, I kept my schedule, I carried out my responsibilities, but I wonder Lord, in your sight did I accomplish anything worthwhile?

Did I enjoy the journey?
Did I value this precious and unique day?
Did I give more than I received?
Did I reach out to persons with genuine love and concern?
Did I treat others as I would like to be treated?

I confess that I'm often a poor witness for you. I miss opportunities to serve you. I get caught up in my own world. I fail to express love to those who need it the most, and I'm not very good at encouraging and affirming those around me.

Lord, you know where I need to change. Enable me to become more passionate about living. Help me to be open to your Spirit. Instill within me a deeper appreciation of the life you have given me. Make me more loving, more caring, more aware, more alive!

I realize there is much to do and much to become - in your hands my life has great possibility. Now, let me sleep soundly, peacefully, and well. In Jesus' name. Amen.

DAY 14   NOTES, REFLECTIONS, PRAYER REQUESTS

COURAGE

God, you created me, and made me to be like yourself.
I don't know exactly what that means, except that I have
longings and needs only you can satisfy.
I reach,
I wonder,
I pray,
I hope,
I dream,
I love.

But sometimes it seems that I reach for nothing; my wonder
dries up; I forget to pray; my hope evaporates; my dreams
disappear; and my love is put to the test.   Lord, deliver me
from being discouraged; lift up my heart.

Through this new day keep me strong and purposeful. Help
me to walk with courage. Make me faithful to you in every
circumstance, and no matter what life brings, keep me
positive and hopeful.

Enable me to trust you, to believe in you, to love you in rain
or shine, in warmth or cold, in crisis or calm.

Now go with me into this day, Lord, and give me a loving
heart like Jesus. Amen.

HELP

Lord of life, some days are interrupted by delays, dilemmas, detours, and disappointments. Today was no different. Things did not always go as planned. At times I was not very patient, and there were moments when I completely forgot who I was and whose I was.

As the day comes to close, help me work through those things that were hard and challenging.

Come, Heavenly Father; come, Lord Jesus; come, Holy Spirit, into this life that I'm trying to manage. Come with your strength and love and give me your guidance and care.

I pray for all who are struggling with life. Help those who are battered and bruised, those who feel defeated and without hope. Wrap your loving arms around them and around me. Heal our hurts, and give us your comfort. Let new hope come to us all.

In the stillness of this night, I surrender my will to your will. Forgive me for what is past and prepare me for what is to come. And now, let me sleep in peace knowing that you are with me always. Amen.

God is our refuge and strength, a very present help in trouble.

Psalm 46:1

SHINE

God, who dwells in this life with us, as I go into this newly made day, let your light shine in and through my very ordinary life.

Let me stand up
>for that which is pure, just, and good,
>for truth and honesty,
>for right over wrong,
>for being responsible and dependable,
>for you and for Jesus Christ.

Today
>let me put helping others above satisfying self;
>let me put giving above taking;
>let me put doing the right thing above the quick fix;
>let me put persons above things;
>let me put you first in my life.

Use me as your servant, God. Give me a desire to reach out to all persons including the lonely, the least, and the lost. For Jesus' sake. Amen.

Very truly, I tell you, unless a grain of wheat dies, it remains just a single grain; but if it dies, it bears much fruit.

John 12:24

DAY 15   NOTES, REFLECTIONS, PRAYER REQUESTS

ALONE

Loving God, sometimes I feel so alone, as if nobody cares. I feel empty on the inside - far from your presence. I feel separated and isolated from other people. I feel exposed and vulnerable, like a turtle without its shell. Everything is black, and I don't know what to do.

Help me!
Deliver me from my despair.
Bring color back into my life.
Give me someone to confide in.
Wrap your loving arms around me.
Help me to get through this difficult time.

Hold me close to you through this night,
    and take care of me.
I place myself in your hands.
Soothe my soul and give me peace.
I am yours and yours alone. Amen.

Why are you cast down, O my soul,
And why are you disquieted within me?
Hope in God; for I shall again praise him,
My help and my God.

                            Psalm 42:11

DAY 16   NOTES, REFLECTIONS, PRAYER REQUESTS

EMPOWER

Lord, thank you for getting me through the night and for a fresh new day. I've been deflated. Help me to get myself back together. Prepare me for that which is to come. Arm me with your love. Equip me with your strength, and lead me into this day with courage and confidence.

God, I'm going to need your help
    To tackle my responsibilities,
    To overcome any self-doubt, fear, or anxiety,
    To give love and friendship to others,
    To accomplish what I need to do with swift certainty.

The day ahead looks like a huge mountain to climb, but help me to begin step by step as you guide me. Empower me, Lord, and keep me moving forward. For yours is the kingdom of light and hope and joy. Amen.

Be strong and courageous; do not be frightened or dismayed, for the Lord your God is with you wherever you go.
Joshua 1:9

ENCOURAGE

Gracious God, as the day comes to a close, I am grateful for the way you care for me from day to day.

You encourage me to do my best,
You sustain me in the tough times,
You lead me through my wilderness moments,
You love me always, even when I am not very lovable,
You give me family and friends to love and to be loved by,
You provide for my every need,
And most of all, you give me a Savior.

I know my life is not always as it should be and that I sometimes make mistakes and say and do the wrong thing, but I'm thankful that you keep working with me.

Lord, I'm tremendously grateful for all you have done and are doing in my life and for seeing me through another day. In the name of Jesus. Amen.

DAY 17   NOTES, REFLECTIONS, PRAYER REQUESTS

FOLLOW

Loving God, I often search for joy and love in all the wrong places. Deep down I know that to be fulfilled I need to be in a right relationship with you. You are the source of joy and love, and the closer I am to you the more joyful and the more loving I will be.

As I encounter life, I sometimes wonder again what your will is for me. What do you want me to do? What do you want me to be? What is your plan and purpose for my life?

In response
You say, "Follow me."
You say, "Deny yourself."
You say, "I am the way."
You say, "You shall love the Lord your God with all your heart, and with all your soul, and with all your mind."

You are Lord! Let me be your obedient servant. I am willing to go wherever you want me to go and do whatever you want me to do. Today help me to follow you without question or reservation. Through Jesus Christ. Amen.

Quotes are found in the following Scriptures:
Matthew 4:19, Mark 10:37, John 14:6, Matthew 22:37-40

DAY 17   NOTES, REFLECTIONS, PRAYER REQUESTS

HOLY

Holy, holy, holy, only you are holy. I wish I could be more holy, God, more of the person you created me to be, less of the person I often am.

I say things;
I think things;
I do things that separate me from you and from others.

Deliver me from an unholy life. I want to please you in the way I live.

> Enable me to think healthy and clean thoughts.
> Make my words gracious, kind, and true.
> Remove any unworthy desire or any resentment
> I may feel toward another.
> Let my love be sincere and accepting.
> Take away any selfish pride or pretense.
> Bring healing to my fragmented and fractured life.

Lord, I entrust my family and friends into your care, especially ...

Give comfort to those who are feeling discouraged and help to those who are trying to make it from one day to the next. Keep watch over all of us through this night and give us your peace. In the name of Jesus, your Son and my Savior. Amen.

DAY 18   NOTES, REFLECTIONS, PRAYER REQUESTS

OPENNESS

God, at times life seems almost overwhelming. There is so much to do, so much to be, and life is often a place filled with trouble and unrest. There is so much violence, so much brokenness, so much emptiness and apathy, so much hurry and rushing about.

Sometimes, I run into dead-end streets, and I don't know what to do or where to turn. In those moments, make a way where there is no way.

Open new doors.
Open windows of opportunity.
Open my life to the stirring of your Spirit.

As I live this day, remove any anxiety from within me, and infuse my whole being with your transforming love and awesome power. Let me make a positive difference.

You know the persons I need to see and the places I need to go. I am at your disposal. Use me as you will. For Christ's sake. Amen.

I sought the Lord, and he heard me; and he delivered me from all my troubles.

Psalm 34:4

DAY 18   NOTES, REFLECTIONS, PRAYER REQUESTS

UNDERNEATH

Most holy God, it touches me when I realize the height and depth of your love for me, and how you desire for me to love you with all my heart.

I confess that I sometimes slip into playing the part of being someone other than myself, and I'm sorry.

I can be the great pretender
Pretending to know it all,
Pretending like I don't need you,
Pretending to be better than I really am,
Pretending to have all the answers,
Pretending to be so high and mighty.

But as you know, underneath the facade I'm simply a struggling sinner. On my worst days, I'm someone who can be pulled from your love and from your presence.

I confess to you, Lord, my sins. Take away any hypocrisy or impurity within me and through your mercy make my heart clean and pure again.

In quiet surrender, I give myself to you. Amen.

DAY 19   NOTES, REFLECTIONS, PRAYER REQUESTS

NOURISH

Bread, that's what you called yourself, God. Jesus said, *I am the bread of life.** I'm hungry for the bread you offer. I'm in need of more nourishment. I long for more of your love, for more of you in my life. Daily pursuits drain my energy. Problems sap my strength. Stress eats me up on the inside.

Holy Bread, fill the empty places within me, clean up the dirty places, satisfy the hungry places, heal the broken places.

The world offers cotton candy; pretty and sweet to the taste, but full of air and emptiness. I need something more; something more substantial; something more lasting.

Often, I sin. I give in to the shallow, the cheap, the trivial, the superficial, and the instantaneous. But they have little value, and they leave me feeling unhappy, unfulfilled, and unsatisfied.

Lord, I desire more of you. You are the bread that gives life. Nourish my soul and renew my strength.

As I go into this day, give me courage and the desire to share what I have received from you with those who are hungering and thirsting for something more. In the name of Jesus. Amen.

*John 6:35

DAY 19   NOTES, REFLECTIONS, PRAYER REQUESTS

FOCUS

God of the day and the night, hear me and help me. I wanted to live today in a way that was pleasing to you, and to convey your love in my words and in my actions. I know that I didn't always accomplish that.

There were times
When I made mistakes,
When I became distracted,
When I was preoccupied with my own needs,
When I did not listen to your voice or walk in your way.
I'm sorry. Forgive me.

I struggle with all that goes on each day. In the midst of living, strengthen me and help me to be as loving and caring as I possibly can be.

In those moments when I don't know what to do or where to go or to whom to turn, enable me to put my hand in your hand, and surrender my will to your will. There I am safe and loved.

Now, God, clear my mind of the day's worries and regrets. Free me from disturbing thoughts and dreams. And if I have trouble sleeping, keep me focused on the good. In Jesus' name. Amen.

DAY 20   Notes, Reflections, Prayer Requests

BELIEVE

God, in a world that is filled with much uncertainty, I believe you love me, and that you want me to love you back. I believe you are with me always. I believe, Lord; help me in my moments of unbelief.

I believe in you.
I believe Jesus is your Son.
I believe in the Holy Spirit, your presence with me.
I believe that good is stronger than evil.

Help me to keep believing, to keep trusting you, to keep following you in every situation. As I begin this day, I place myself, and my loved ones in your hands.

Open my life to your will and way. I believe! Thank you for believing in me. Now let me go into this day with fearless faith. I ask these things in the name of Jesus, my Lord and Savior. Amen.

****

I believe in the sun
even when it is not shining.
I believe in love
even when I feel it not.
I believe in God
even when he is silent.

(These words were scrawled on a cellar wall where Jews had hidden in World War II in Cologne, Germany)

FRAGILE

Loving God, life is so unpredictable, and things can quickly change. Accidents can happen. Illness can strike us down. A crisis or tragedy can befall us. Devastating news may come our way. We are caught off guard and are left feeling bewildered and overwhelmed. Life suddenly takes on a deeper meaning and becomes very fragile.

As changes come into my life, God, help me not to lose heart but to trust in you. You are more powerful than anything that will ever happen to me. In you there is strength; in you there is healing; in you there is hope; and in you there is life now and forever.

No matter what happens,
Keep me faithful;
Keep me believing;
Keep me open to new possibilities;
Keep me positive about the present and the future.

I pray for those in my family and for my friends. Keep them in your care and guide them through each day and night. Wrap your loving arms around them and me, and give us all strength and courage.

Thank you, Lord, for being there for me and for your gracious love in this life and the life to come. Now, calm my fears and keep me close to you. In the name of your dear Son. Amen.

But we have this treasure in earthen vessels, to show that the transcendent power belongs to God and not to us. We are afflicted in every way, but not crushed; perplexed, but not driven to despair, persecuted but not forsaken; struck down, but not destroyed...

2 Corinthians 4:7-9

DAY 21   NOTES, REFLECTIONS, PRAYER REQUESTS

INSTRUMENT

God of glory, as I launch out into this new day, I need you in my life. I need you to guide me in the way I need to go.

Through this day there will be
Decisions to make,
Responsibilities to face,
Problems to solve,
Crises to handle,
Conflicts to settle,
Goals to strive after,
Relationships to strengthen and more of the unexpected.

Lord, help me!

Let me be attentive to your Spirit, responsive to your leading, and sensitive to others.

Make me an instrument of your love and peace in all that I say, in all that I do, and in all that I seek to be. For Jesus' sake, Amen.

God be in my head, and in my understanding;
God be in my eyes, and in my looking;
God be in my mouth, and in my speaking;
God be in my heart, and in my thinking;
God be at my end, and at my departing.

Sarum Liturgy, England, 13th Century

DAY 21   NOTES, REFLECTIONS, PRAYER REQUESTS

REGRET

Father, you have watched over my life with endless love and care, and guided me through this day.

Thank you
  for loving me without condition,
  for helping me when I cannot help myself,
  for strength in times of trouble,
  for allowing me to serve you.

I regret those times
  When I lost my direction,
  When I put off doing what needed to be done,
  When I missed helping someone in need,
  When I indulged in pursuits that were not good for me.

Lord, forgive me, and help me to begin again tomorrow.

Care for my family, my friends, and for me through this night, and let us all rest and relax in your unchanging and renewing love. Amen.

DAY 22   NOTES, REFLECTIONS, PRAYER REQUESTS

WONDER

Ever-present God, it is so good to be alive!
To breathe,
To feel,
To touch,
To see,
To hear,
To speak,
To think,
To love and be loved,
To walk,
To run,
To smile,
To laugh,
To dream,
To dance.

O the wonder of it all!

Lord, as I go through this day, help me to treasure each moment, even the most difficult ones.

Empty me of self and fill me with your Spirit. Let me share my love and myself joyfully and generously with every person I meet. In your Son's name. Amen.

DAY 22   NOTES, REFLECTIONS, PRAYER REQUESTS

INTENTION

God, as the day gently comes to an end, I turn to you. I remember how I set out this morning with joy in my heart, peace in my soul, and the best of intentions.

I tried to give love;
I tried to be patient;
I tried to be thoughtful;
I tried to be sensitive to those around me.

But at times all of that went amiss.
I ended up withholding love;
I became irritated;
I lost sight of what I needed to do for others; and
I became wrapped up in my own needs and could see no further.

Lord, bless and expand the good I did today, and if I caused any harm or hurt, cancel and diminish it by your power. Make me a better person. Enable me to be more consistent in my loving and in my caring. Help me not to give up on myself, but to allow you to keep changing me from within.

I entrust my family, my friends, my co-workers, and myself to your care. Calm our fears and supply our needs. In Jesus' name. Amen.

DAY 23   NOTES, REFLECTIONS, PRAYER REQUESTS

STRENGTH

Loving God, in whom I live and move and have my being, life is wonderful and life is difficult. Some days it is full of absolute wonder, and I thank you for it. On those days I feel joyfully alive and full of unwavering faith. But on other days, life is demanding and extremely hard, and it can cause me to feel down and discouraged. Problems wear me out, and stress drains me.

For the easier days, give me a grateful heart. For the difficult ones, give me strength, courage, and enough faith to get through them.

For this particular new day, give me whatever I need to live it in a way that pleases you. Enable me to make room for others in the circle of my life and in the circle of my caring. Don't let me overlook anyone in the busyness of this day.

Lead me over the ups and through the downs. Whatever the day brings let me handle it with sensitivity and understanding. Let it be a good day as I place my life in your strong hands. I ask this in the name of Jesus Christ, to whom be glory and honor forever and ever. Amen.

MERCY

Lord, you were with me today. You were aware of my thoughts, you sensed my feelings, and you know my hopes and dreams. You heard my words; you saw what I did and what I failed to do.

You keep giving me opportunities to do better. Help me to take advantage of them.

When I see someone in need, show me how to express care and help to that person. When occasions to serve are presented, guide me in using the gifts and talents you've given me.

Pick me up and move me to where I need to be. Teach me to love more, to trust you more, and to surrender more of my life to you. Help me to stand up for the way you call me to live and not give in to anything less.

Have mercy on me. Have mercy on me, most merciful Savior, and see me safely through this night. Amen.

DAY 24   NOTES, REFLECTIONS, PRAYER REQUESTS

Receptive

You are the alpha and the omega, the beginning and the end. You are a mighty God. In Jesus you are the vine and we are the branches. Through him you are beautiful Savior, the Resurrection, and the Life.

Lord, that's what I need—life, new, pulsating life! Don't let me stay as I am. Don't let me give in to the demons of darkness and despair, of fear and discouragement.

Set me free from those things that bind me. Keep me moving forward as I discover this brand new day.

Warm my refrigerated heart, and make me receptive to your Holy Spirit. Instill in me the desire to live for you and for Jesus and not just for myself.

Change me from caterpillar into butterfly. Teach me to live more daringly, more expectantly, more joyfully as a follower of Jesus.

Take my hand and lead me through this day. And when my earthly life is over, take my hand again and lead me into your heavenly kingdom. In the name of the living Christ. Amen.

RENEW

God, as the shadows of the evening fall and I come to the end of this day, take my tired, worn out body and renew it with satisfying rest.

The remains of the day are still with me. Help me to lay down my burdens and to release my cares and concerns to you.

Take from my mind reoccurring thoughts and incessant worries over what I have done or left undone. Forgive me of any sin I may have committed through my own carelessness or neglect, and help me to be forgiving of others.

Lord, I rejoice that you love me, and that you give me new opportunities to serve you more fully.

As I lie down in peace, let me fear no evil, but confidently give my loved ones and myself into your keeping; through Jesus Christ my Lord. Amen.

Cast your burden on the Lord, and he will sustain you.
                                                    Psalm 55:22

DAY 25   NOTES, REFLECTIONS, PRAYER REQUESTS

SERVICE

God of my life, I welcome this new day; your gift to me. I often begin this time of prayer by telling you what I need. But this morning, I'd like to ask, what can I do for you?

Enable me
To put you first in all things,
To love you totally,
To give love freely and graciously,
To speak with you often,
To serve you and others,
To obey you,
To share what I have,
To completely trust you.

Lord, you helped Nehemiah build a wall in 52 days.* Help me to build a life that is pleasing to you; one that reflects your self-giving love and your constant goodness.

If I begin to stray from you, to complain, to find fault, to want my own way, forgive me, and put me right with you as quickly as possible.

Through this day, help me to feel your presence in a very real way. In the name of your Son. Amen.

*Nehemiah 6:15

DAY 25   Notes, Reflections, Prayer Requests

GIFT

God, I've been thinking about this day, this unique gift that you placed in my hands and how I lived it.

There were the good things I wanted to do -
Encourage others,
Love unselfishly,
Listen with my heart,
Refrain from judging,
Be wise in matters of concern,
Speak the right words,
Stay calm.

But then, there were the things that I actually did -
Put someone down,
Loved selectively,
Talked too much,
Judged others,
Made foolish comments,
Displayed a sharp tongue,
Lost my temper.

Forgive me. I give myself to you; make me new again. As tomorrow comes, I am grateful that you are working in and through me to make me better than I am. Good night, Lord. Amen.

DAY 26 NOTES, REFLECTIONS, PRAYER REQUESTS

COPE

Some days, God, I begin wondering if I have enough strength to cope with another day. The sun rises, and the day comes with a rush. Suddenly there are tasks to do, people to see, errands to run, calls to make, and persons to love and serve.

Some days there are situations to work through and hurt feelings to mend. Life becomes consuming and demanding, and I'm carried along with its flow. Much of what comes before me will require wisdom, understanding, and lots of patience.

In the midst of it all, I sometimes forget that I do not have to face life alone. You are with me! You are right here with me, and that makes all the difference. You are in the here and now, upholding me with your Holy Spirit, and wherever this day takes me you will be right there -- guiding, encouraging, helping, comforting. And I need not be afraid!

So, no matter what the day brings, Lord, I know without a doubt that you and I can handle it together. Thank you for your living presence that is with me through this day and always. Amen.

I can do all things through Christ who strengthens me.
Philippians 4:13

TOMORROW

Loving God, after the activities of this day I feel exhausted. My energy is gone and my strength used up. Today was demanding and at times challenging, but it was also good and fulfilling.

As I made decisions and carried out responsibilities, I trust that they were done in accordance with your will. There were times when I had to act quickly and do what I thought was the right and loving thing. Lord, if I made any bad moves or misjudgments, have mercy on me.

I look forward to tomorrow. Prepare me for it. Re-energize and strengthen my life. Renew my zest for living, and let me be touched by your living and moving Spirit.

To your loving care, Heavenly Father, I commend all those who are dear to me, especially...

For those who are wrestling with some concern, some upheaval in their lives, provide your care, and enable all of us to sleep in peace. In the name of Christ. Amen.

WITNESS

Lord of this new day, I lift my heart to you in praise and adoration. You make me happy. You make life worth living. You surround me with a great cloud of witnesses—those who have finished the race and gone before me.* They are in the bleachers cheering me on. Through this day let me hear their shouts of love, support, and encouragement.

Even though I want to be your witness here, I can easily get distracted and become too focused on myself. My light can become a little flicker. It loses its power and influence for your good.

Keep my life centered on you. Make my light strong and bright so that others may see your goodness and love reflected through me.

I know I will have opportunities today to make a positive difference for you. Help me to listen not only with my ears, but with my heart; to see not only with my eyes, but with a sensitive spirit.

Let me hear again the shouts of those victorious witnesses, and be encouraged to serve you faithfully. Through Jesus my Lord. Amen.

*Hebrews 12:1-2

DAY 27   N<small>OTES,</small> R<small>EFLECTIONS,</small> P<small>RAYER</small> R<small>EQUESTS</small>

RESHAPE

God, as you know, even on my best days life can be a real struggle. Today I was able to accomplish much. You gave me joy and meaning, and I am grateful. But all was not as it should be. There were times when I pulled back, when I gave in, when I stopped short, and failed to live up your expectations.

Breathe new life into me. Lift me up and set my feet on solid ground. You are the potter; I am the clay. Reshape and remake me. You have equipped me to be a noble creature. Give me a vision of my best self. Bring healing to the brokenness and hurt within me, and let me walk with my head up, strengthened and comforted by your abiding presence.

Spirit of the living God,
Fall afresh on me.
Spirit of the living God,
Fall afresh on me.
Melt me, mold me,
Fill me, use me.
Spirit of the living God,
*Fall afresh on me.**

Now bring quiet to my mind and sleep to my body. In the wondrous name of Jesus. Amen.

*Hymn: Spirit of the Living God by Daniel Iverson

DAY 28   NOTES, REFLECTIONS, PRAYER REQUESTS

OPPORTUNITIES

God, you created this one-of-a-kind day; it's fresh, bright, open-ended, and ready to be lived. I thank you for it! It's also full of challenges and opportunities. Help me not draw back from it, but, in your strength, let me seize the day - carpe diem! Let me meet it with steady faith, a cheerful spirit, and a sense of eager anticipation.

Of course, I know that there will be
    Obstacles to overcome,
    Interruptions to handle,
    Decisions to make,
    And problems to solve.

Help me with whatever comes my way.

There will also be persons to deal with;
Some will be cooperative and friendly;
Others will be hard and difficult.
Some will be trusting; others suspicious;
Some will be happy, and others upset.

Enable me to relate to each person in the most loving way. In all that I do, give me extra patience and understanding.

As I serve you, let me live this day to its fullest and let me live it with joy. In the name of Jesus. Amen.

CHANCE

As I come to this time of prayer, God, I feel exhausted. It has been a long and trying day, and at times, I felt like I let you down and myself, as well.

There were moments when
I reacted instead of responding,
I said words too quickly and too sharply,
I fueled a bad attitude,
I had an unwillingness to bear the burdens of others,
I neglected occasions to do good,
I missed the mark of your high calling.

I am grateful that you are a forgiving God and that you do not hold my sins against me. Let me move beyond sorrow over what I have done to joy in your goodness. Let my disappointment in my actions be left behind as I give myself anew to you. Thank you, Heavenly Father, for giving me another chance to prove myself.

Now, calm my heart and mind and let me sleep peacefully and well. For Jesus' sake. Amen.

DAY 29   NOTES, REFLECTIONS, PRAYER REQUESTS

AFFIRM

God of the stars, sun, and moon and the galaxies beyond, your world is so big and I am so small. Often, I feel insignificant and inadequate. But you affirm the person I am and the gifts I possess, and in my weakness you make me strong.

You know all about me –
my past,
my fears,
my shortcomings,
my sins,
and you still love me completely.
Thank you for caring so much about me – all the time –
even when I am not at my best.

Forgive me for my reluctance to let you have your way in my life. Fill me with the desire to be shaped by you in every facet of who I am. Through this day, help me to live according to your way – not mine. In the name of the indwelling Christ I pray. Amen.

Are not five sparrows sold for two pennies? And not one of them is forgotten before God. Why, even the hairs of your head are all numbered. Fear not; you are of more value that many sparrows.

Luke 12:6-7

DAY 29   NOTES, REFLECTIONS, PRAYER REQUESTS

ACCOUNTABLILITY

Father, in this time of quiet, I wonder about my life. As I deal with everyday things, I realize I need to look more carefully at the way I'm living. It's not easy for me to evaluate myself – to really see myself as I am. I need you to help me and to walk with me.

I ask
Do I keep my promises?
Do I always tell the whole truth?
Do I convey sufficient love to my family and friends?
Do I express enough concern for my co-workers?
Do I stand up for my values and convictions?
Do I offer words of encouragement?
Do I resist temptation?
Do I serve others willingly?

Remind me of the little things that I need to do in order to say yes to these questions. Help me to be open and sensitive to your leading.

I've come a long way, but I have miles to go. Keep refining my life. Keep me accountable. Keep me growing in my relationship with you.

As I lie down to sleep, I entrust my family and friends and myself to your watchful care. In Jesus' name. Amen.

DAY 30   NOTES, REFLECTIONS, PRAYER REQUESTS

INCREASE

Good morning, Lord. Help me to live this day with joy and eager expectation and not let the things of the world get in the way.

Increase my faith.
Some days my faith seems weak and uncertain. Life begins to crowd in on me, and I don't know which way to turn. Whenever that occurs, help me to hold on to you, and to live by faith!

Increase my hope.
Sometimes life causes me to feel hopeless. It beats me down; it produces despair and discouragement within me. Whenever that darkness comes, don't let me give in or give up. Keep me hopeful!

Increase my love.
Some days I have such difficulty giving love. Lord, every person I meet today is longing for love and for someone to truly care about him or her. Enable me to love that person. Make me more loving!

Now, let me go into this day with my eyes and heart wide open and ready to share what I have discovered in you. I ask these things in the strong name of Jesus. Amen.

DAY 30   NOTES, REFLECTIONS, PRAYER REQUESTS

RELATIONSHIPS

Loving God, I am grateful that this day has nearly run its course, and I thank you for your constant love and care of my life.

As I revisit this day in my mind, I think about my relationship with others, and how I responded to the people around me. Sometimes I responded in a good and helpful way; other times I responded poorly or not at all.

There were times
> when I was so engrossed in what I was doing that
> I didn't notice the needs of those around me;
> when I made a hurtful comment toward another;
> when I ignored my neighbor and passed by on the other side.

Have mercy on me, and keep working in my life until I get it right. Teach me to be more aware. When I'm with someone, help me to give that person my complete and undivided attention and to really be present in that moment.

Now, as I lie down to sleep, take from me the strain and stress of the day and refresh me in body, mind, and spirit. In the Savior's name. Amen.

DAY 31   NOTES, REFLECTIONS, PRAYER REQUESTS

DISCIPLE

God, help me to deal with life as it comes today. It is often like a roller coaster, full of sharp turns, dark tunnels, and unexpected ups and downs. When the unknown and the unexpected come, let me be ready.

Make me a daring disciple of Jesus. Send me out of this place into the mission field, which begins right outside my front door. Place in my heart a desire to reach out to friends, to strangers, and to everyone with love and kindness.

I don't feel daring. I'm not good at sharing my faith. It's hard for me to get out of my comfort zone. But I'm willing if you will help me. Show me how to care enough to move beyond my self-imposed limitations. Love others through me. Enable me to be a channel of your grace.

Lord, use me in the best possible way. Lead on, and I will follow. Amen.

And they'll know we are Christians by our love, by our love; yes, they'll know we are Christians by our love.
From hymn by Peter Scholtes

DAY 31   NOTES, REFLECTIONS, PRAYER REQUESTS

HEALING

Gracious God, 1 appreciate the life you've given me, and I thank you for the privilege of living it. Thank you for guiding me safely through another day and for caring for me through this night.

On my journey, I have come to realize that there are some things I need to keep giving up and letting go. They cling to me like incrusted barnacles. They drag me down and get in the way of my living.

You know what they are. I've lived with them for quite a while. This night set me free from those things that still haunt me –

> Unforgotten failures,
> Broken dreams,
> Old hurts,
> Bitter disappointments,
> Buried feelings.

Take these things from me, and cast them into the deepest part of the sea. And in their place bring healing, wholeness, and peace to my life. Through your transforming love, help me to move into the future as a better and stronger person.

Now quiet my mind and heart, and as I sleep, take away my weariness. In your Son's name. Amen.

APPENDIX

*Particularly
Meaningful Prayers*

SUNDAY - MORNING

Loving God, thank you for the privilege of worship and the opportunity to give you my praise, my thankfulness, and myself.

Let me experience your presence and hear your voice through the music, the praying, the silences, the reading of the Scripture, the giving of gifts, and the preaching of your Word. Speak through those who lead us.

You are an awesome God! You love me without condition. You abundantly provide for my needs. You guide and uphold my life. You give me joy and a peace that the world cannot take away.

Make me conscious of those around me and enable me to share with them what I have found in you.

Through worship
Refresh and renew my life,
Repair the damaged places,
Heal the broken places,
Make straight the crooked places,
Keep changing me into the person you created me to be.

Now, let me go to serve you. Use my hands, my eyes, my feet, my voice, my heart, all of me, to help those in my home, in my neighborhood, in my community, and in your world. Let me be your light wherever I am.

For Christ's sake. Amen.

SUNDAY - MORNING

Joyful, joyful we adore thee, God of glory, Lord of love*

Almighty God, unto whom all hearts are open, all desires known, and from whom no secrets are hid: Cleanse the thoughts of our hearts by the inspiration of your Holy Spirit, that we may perfectly love you, and worthily magnify your holy name; through Christ our Lord.**

Lord, thank you for the privilege of offering myself to you through worship. As I worship you refresh my spirit and renew my faith.

Today I ask you bless and encourage all those who willingly and devotedly serve you this day...pastors, teachers, musicians, church staff, missionaries, youth counselors, nursery attendants, ushers, greeters, helpers, and other servants. Use each one as a channel of your transforming love.

I pray for those who are persecuted for their faith. Give them strength and courage as they bear witness to you and to Jesus.

Help those who are experiencing great trouble today. In the midst of their darkness and despair, give them new hope to keep on going.

Now, as I enter into worship give me a receptive spirit. Touch my heart, change my life, and to you be all praise and glory. In the name of your Son and my Savior. Amen.

* From the hymn *Joyful, Joyful, Lord, We Adore Thee*
   Words: Henry Van Dyke
**The Collect for Purity
   The Book of Common Prayer (1979)

Dear Jesus,

Help me to spread your fragrance everywhere I go.

Flood my soul with your spirit and life.

Penetrate and possess my whole being so utterly that
my life may only be a radiance of yours.

Shine through me
and be so in me
that every soul I come in contact with
may feel your presence in my soul.

Let them look up and see no longer me
but only Jesus.

Stay with us
and then I shall begin to shine as you shine,
so to shine as to be light to others.

The light, O Jesus, will be all from you.

None of it will be mine.

It will be your shining on others through me.

Let me thus praise you in the way you love best
by shining on those around me.... Amen.

Mother Teresa of Calcutta (1910-1997)

O Holy Spirit,
Come into my heart and fill me.
I open wide all the windows of my soul to let you in.
Come and possess me completely.
Fill me with your light and truth.
I offer you the only thing I really possess –
My capacity to be filled with and by you.

Of myself I am an unprofitable servant,
An empty vessel,
To be consecrated, filled, and used for your purpose.
Fill me so that I may live the life of your Spirit,
The life of truth and goodness,
The life of beauty, love, and joy,
The life of wisdom and strength.

Guide me today in all things,
Guide me to the people I should meet or help,
To the circumstances in which I can best serve you
Whether by my actions or by my sufferings.
But above all let Christ be formed in me—
That I may dethrone self in my heart and make Him king.
Bind and cement me to Christ by all your ways,
Known and unknown;
By holy thoughts and unseen graces
And sacramental ties,
So that He abides in me and I abide in Him,
Today and forever.
Amen.

Walter J. Carey
Anglican Bishop of Bloemfontein (1923)

O God, early in the morning I cry to you.
Help me to pray
And to concentrate my thoughts on you:
I cannot do this alone.

In me there is darkness,
But with you there is light;
I am lonely, but you do not leave me;
I am feeble in heart, but with you there is help;
I am restless, but with you there is peace.
In me there is bitterness, but with you there is patience;
I do not understand your ways,
But you know the way for me...

Restore me to liberty,
And enable me so to live now
That I may answer before you and before me.
Lord, whatever this day may bring,
Your name be praised.

Dietrich Bonhoeffer (1906-1945)
(German theologian and anti-Nazi who wrote this prayer
while awaiting execution)

Lord, make me an instrument of your peace,
Where there is hatred, let me sow love;
Where there is injury, pardon;
Where there is doubt, faith;
Where there is despair, hope;
Where is darkness, light;
Where there is sadness, joy.

O Divine Master,
Grant that I may not so much seek to be consoled
as to console; to be understood as to understand;
to be loved as to love.

For it is in giving that we receive;
it is in pardoning that we are pardoned;
and it is in dying that we are born to eternal life.

St. Francis of Assisi
(1182-1226)

17th Century Nun's Prayer

Lord, thou knowest better than I know myself that I am growing older and will someday be old. Keep me from the fatal habit of thinking I must say something on every subject and on every occasion. Release me from craving to straighten out everybody's affairs. Make me thoughtful but not moody; helpful but not bossy. With my vast store of wisdom, it seems a pity not to use it all, but Thou knowest Lord that I want a few friends at the end.

Keep my mind free from the recital of endless details; give me wings to get to the point. Seal my lips on my aches and pains. They are increasing, and love of rehearsing them is becoming sweeter as the years go by. I dare not ask for grace enough to enjoy the tales of others' pains, but help me to endure them with patience.

I dare not ask for improved memory, but for a growing humility and a lessening cocksureness when my memory seems to clash with the memories of others. Teach me the glorious lesson that occasionally I may be mistaken.

Keep me reasonably sweet; I do not want to be a Saint—some of them are so hard to live with—but a sour old person is one of the crowning works of the devil. Give me the ability to see good things in unexpected places, and talents in unexpected people. And give me, O Lord, the grace to tell them so. Amen.